Feed Sack Dresses

and

Wild Plum Jam

Remembering
Farm Life
in the 1950s

BY MARILYN KRATZ

Remember the good days!

Marilyn Kratz

Oct. 24, 2013

prairie hearth
publishing, llc

ISBN: 978-1491091074

Cover Design by Melanie Bender

Copyedited by Kathy K. Grow, www.DoWriteEditing.com

Line drawings are illustrations of South Dakota wildflowers, United States Department of Agriculture

First printing August 2013

Published by:
Prairie Hearth Publishing, LLC
PO Box 569
Yankton, SD 57078

DEDICATION

I dedicate this book to the memory of my parents, Martha and Oscar Thum, who made my childhood a pleasant place to remember, and to my brother, Marvin, and sisters, Viona and Donna, who lived these memories with me.

Thanks to Loretta Sorensen for helping this book come to be, to my niece Melanie Bender for designing the perfect cover, and to my husband, Bud, for his loving support in all my endeavors.

INTRODUCTION

As we grow older, we often think fondly of times, places, and people we knew as children. Those days were days of carefree joy. We didn't realize wearing dresses made from feed sacks indicated our parents couldn't afford "store-bought" dresses. We didn't think about all the work that went into having good, wholesome, homegrown food on the table. We were comfortable in a world where we understood how almost everything worked.

As you read this collection of my memories of growing up on a small farm in southeastern South Dakota, I hope they take you back to beloved sacred places in your own memories.

Table of Contents

Author is shown, far right, with brother Marvin and sister Viona.
The girls wear homemade dresses.

The Dress Grandma Made

New clothes were a rare treat in my childhood. I was happy with anything new Mama sewed for me or even any hand-me-downs I could get.

Then, one day, when I was about eight years old, my school friends Margaret and Georgine wore their new store-bought dresses with full circle skirts to our one-room rural schoolhouse. I longed to have such a dress. No matter how I tried to pull all the fullness in my skirt to one side of my seat, not one of my homemade feed sack dresses had the fullness of those magnificent circle skirts.

Soon after that, Grandma offered to make me a new feed sack dress. I chose a pink-flowered print and asked Mama if Grandma could make my new dress with a circle skirt. Mama reminded me that there wasn't much material in one feed sack. But, as I waited impatiently for my new dress, I couldn't help dreaming of twirling around in it and having the skirt flare out in a rippling circle around me.

I pictured myself standing on the floor grate of the school's coal furnace while rising air made my skirt float up like an open umbrella. Most of all, I pictured myself sitting at my desk with my skirt draping to the floor on *both* sides of my seat, just like Margaret's and Georgine's.

At last, the dress was finished. The drive to Grandma's house in town to get it seemed longer than ever before. Then we were standing in Grandma's kitchen. With a proud smile, she held up the flowered pink feed sack dress she had made so lovingly for me. I swallowed a huge lump of disappointment as I spread the skimpy dirndl skirt. Although I was an average-sized eight-year-old, there hadn't been even enough fabric in one feed sack for the entire dress. Grandma had had to make the collar, sleeves, and midriff of matching plain pink fabric.

"How do you like it?" Mama asked, prompting me to give a grateful response.

I can't remember what I said. I hope I thanked Grandma profusely. After all, her labor in making it for me was a gift of love. And it really was a pretty dress, even if it didn't have a full circle skirt.

BACHELOR BUTTON

Farm belonging to author's parents, Oscar and Martha Thum, near
Scotland, South Dakota. Taken in 1974.

Faded Beauty

Boards of narrow siding, gray with age,
Splinter as old barn walls cave in.
You have to imagine the farmer painting them
When they still stood level and firm.
He used the same color each time—Barn Red—
With crisp white trim defining doors and windows.
Now the roof tumbles in,
But you can recall when the farmer took pains
To make sure it was secure against leaks.
You can't smell the dusty hay
Once stacked in the cavernous haymow,
Ready to feed animals all winter long.
You can't even walk inside to see stalls
Where cows waited patiently for milking,
As cats waited around a small stone bowl
To lap up their supper.
Perhaps you can remember the smell of fresh warm milk
Foaming up in the pail
Or the pungent scent of fly spray.

No longer do horses' fly nettings decorate a side wall
In the small room where the cream separator stood.
Maybe, if you let your mind go back,
You can still hear the stamp of horses' hooves
As they waited for the farmer to harness them
For a day's work in fields of ripe oats,
Or the whoosh of cattle breath, as they nuzzled hay.
As you drive on by, try to recall the satisfaction,
The joy, of the farmer long ago
As he stood on the porch of the white frame house
And surveyed his tidy farmyard,
Feeling especially proud of his majestic red barn.
It is still beautiful
Even though its beauty lies not in what now is,
But in what once was.

Drama and Excitement— Right There in Our Kitchen

I stand at the table, slipping skins off homegrown tomatoes Mama has just blanched in boiling water. Sweat pours down my face in the un-air-conditioned kitchen. I sigh as I glance at the pile of tomatoes left for Mama, my sisters, and me to can.

Suddenly, a shout is heard. "I can't stand this any longer!" The sound of sobs is followed by hurried steps across the floor. Then a door slams.

No, neither my sisters nor I have decided we've had it with canning tomatoes. It's just today's episode of a soap opera coming from the big brown radio perched on a shelf in the corner. We continue with the drudgery of canning, but now with our minds off in an entirely different, more exciting, and glamorous world.

One of my favorite dramas was *Judy and Jane*, in which almost every character had a name starting with *J*. Jane's twins were Joel and

Joy. Judy's errant husband was Jerry. Jane's husband was Don, which broke the *J* tradition for some unexplained reason.

I still remember the episode in which Judy asked someone to play Santa Claus for her children. Just as that person arrived in a Santa suit, her often-missing husband Jerry showed up, also in a Santa suit. Only on a soap opera!

Ma Perkins led a life filled with characters as colorful and varied as the products advertised during the commercial breaks in the show. Her dearest friend, who worked at Ma Perkins's lumberyard, was Shuffle Shober.

I pictured her eldest daughter, Evie, flighty and easily excited, with frizzy red hair and bright red orange lipstick. Evie was married to the patient Willy. When Fay, the younger daughter, wept as she did the dishes because she missed her soldier husband, Tom, Ma Perkins said, "It's all right if there's a little salt in the dishwater." How do I remember that particular line after all these years when I can't even remember what I had for lunch today?

The Second Mrs. Burton had to put up with the difficulties of a second marriage in a day when that wasn't as common as it is now. We were always on her side because we knew about the evil invariably being planned by the first Mrs. Burton.

Our Gal Sunday, *The Romance of Helen Trent*, *Portia Faces Life*, and *Young Doctor Malone* drew us daily into lives of people far removed from our home on a prairie farm.

Why do I remember them so vividly? Maybe they were written with more character development and charm than the fast-moving, often brutal series we see on television today.

Perhaps it was because we listened to them, as opposed to watching them. We had to envision the scenes being played out. We imagined how the characters looked, what they wore, and the furniture in their homes. We really came to know and love those long-suffering heroines and heroes.

I wouldn't mind visiting them again today.

BLACK-EYED SUSAN

The Cellar:
A Place to Test My Courage

Just behind our house on the farm where I grew up, a wooden door opened into the side of a small hill. Inside, a set of crumbling cement steps led down to our food cellar, a room about eight- by ten-feet with cement ceiling, walls, and floor, buried two-thirds underground.

Usually when Mama asked me to fetch something from the cellar, I prevailed upon one of my sisters to go with me. But, one day, when Mama needed a jar of peaches, my sisters were off somewhere else, so I had to make the trip down into the cellar alone.

Daddy had punched a small hole through the ceiling of the cellar and lined it with a ceramic cylinder to let in some air. But a metal cap loosely covering it prevented sunlight from dispelling the gloom. I had to find my way with only the light provided by the open door at the top of the stairs.

I kept my eyes on the cracked cement floor as I made my way to wooden shelves along the sides of the room. I made sure to avoid the potatoes we'd piled in one corner.

Mama's crocks of fermenting sauerkraut and watermelon pickles sent out tangy fragrances. I liked those smells. I loved the damp, earthy smell of the cellar even more. But I didn't let those few pleasures keep me down there any longer than I needed to be.

Before reaching up for the jar of peaches, I made sure there were no spider webs nearby. I grabbed the jar and turned to head back up the steps. Then I froze. Between me and the steps, I saw a small spotted lizard peering up at me.

That day, I learned I had more courage than I realized I had. I took a deep breath and headed for the steps, keeping as far away from the lizard as I could. But I will admit to climbing those steps faster than I ever had before!

I can't say that experience cured me completely of my cellar fears. I knew that sometimes a garter snake found its way down there, and that would have scared me even more than a little lizard.

But when storm clouds looked especially threatening, I was always happy to head for the cellar with the rest of the family—and a flashlight. I can't remember doing that too often. Maybe we didn't have many tornadoes back then around our place.

After Daddy added some rooms and a basement to the house, the cellar opened into the far end of the basement. That made it even scarier for me to get a jar of canned goods for Mama. First I'd have to go down into the basement and walk to the darkest corner of that space. Then I'd have to find the courage to enter the cellar. Daddy added a bare light bulb hanging from the top of the cellar after it became an extension of the basement, but it still seemed scary to me.

The cellar always felt cool and damp. But I wasn't tempted to spend any extra time down there, no matter how hot the summer day felt above ground. It was just too strange and spooky, even though it had that wonderful earthy smell.

PASQUE

Party Lines:
Our Way of Keeping in Touch

When I see people talking on cell phones these days, I marvel at how far we've come with such devices. They're just a fraction of the size of the telephones we had in our farm kitchen when I was a girl, and they do many things we couldn't do with ours.

The phone of my past was a brown wooden box about a foot high and probably six inches across and deep. It hung on the wall beside the kitchen cupboards.

On the front were a black mouthpiece and a small shelf to hold a pencil and pad. The receiver hung in a cradle on the left side of the phone box. On the right side was a crank to make the phone ring.

When you wanted to phone someone on your party line, you simply cranked out a set of rings for that household. Each house had its own pattern of rings. Ours was five short rings. When you heard your rings, you picked up the receiver and answered.

If you wanted to phone someone not on your party line, you rang one short ring for the operator. You told her the number you wanted, and she connected your line with that person's line. Then the operator rang the proper number of rings for the person.

A popular habit of party line users was "rubbernecking." That meant listening to other people's calls on your party line. If you heard a set of rings other than your own, you could quietly lift the receiver off the hook and listen in to the conversation. I really believe all the women, and maybe even a lot of men, did that.

I remember one time when a neighbor's wife was having an affair with a chicken feed salesman. He'd call her to make sure her husband wasn't at home before coming out to see her. They used what they were sure was a code so people rubbernecking couldn't figure out what they were actually saying, but all the women in the neighborhood understood exactly what they were planning.

One afternoon when my siblings and I were home alone for a short time, we accidentally put too many cobs in the cookstove and started a chimney fire. In desperation, my brother went to the phone and cranked out some rings. He was too frightened to remember anyone's actual set of rings, but a neighbor answered. My brother quickly explained the situation, and that neighbor's husband came right over to put out the fire before it could do any damage. That day, being on a party line came in really handy.

Because the telephone hung on a wall and could not be taken with us, we didn't do as much phoning as people do nowadays. But, thanks to that party line, we were probably as well informed about things around us as we needed to be. Maybe even a bit more!

Mysterious Objects We Used to Use

If you're like me, you look at all the newfangled items your children and grandchildren use, and you wonder what they are and how they work.

Well, I'm here to tell you, young people nowadays would be just as puzzled if they saw us with some of the gadgets we helped our moms use years ago in the kitchen.

For example, how many children today would know what to do with a wooden board about eighteen inches long and eight inches wide with a set of sharp metal blades inserted diagonally at the center? I remember my mom using that device to shred cabbage to make sauerkraut.

And what would a young person these days do with a long-necked bottle with a cap that had a lot of little holes in it? That's what we used to sprinkle clothes so they'd be just damp enough for us to iron out the wrinkles. Maybe even the iron would puzzle them in this day of wash and wear.

I doubt any youngsters would know what to put into a small metal box with an open trough at the bottom. They'd find it hanging on the wall beside a big brown box only us older people would recognize as a telephone. We would know the small metal box was the place we stored wooden matches we needed to start a fire in the cookstove or light the wicks on kerosene lamps.

Since most kitchens now have microwave ovens, I suspect young cooks no longer need the set of two nested kettles my mom called her double boiler.

Ever hear of the lard bucket? That's where my mom kept any lard left in the pan after frying something. She considered it wasteful to throw it away after just one use. And lard didn't spoil in the kitchen cupboard as it waited to be used again.

How many kitchens still have flour sifters or butter churns? Would today's young cooks know you can tenderize steak by pounding it with the edge of a heavy sauce pan lid? Who needs a fancy meat mallet?

I suspect that, if you showed today's child a rubber ring used to seal canning jars, they'd wonder how we ever made a slingshot with such a stiff "rubber band."

Oh well, to each his own. But I'd rather deal with a pie bird (Google it!) than a smart phone any day.

The Amazing Gas Refrigerator

We had a refrigerator even before we had electricity on the farm where I grew up. It wasn't an icebox like the one I remember my grandma had at her house. Ours was a gas refrigerator.

I've often wondered just how that refrigerator worked since it was powered by burning kerosene in small burners on one side of the big white metal box that contained the cold storage area. I can't remember if they burned continuously, but I remember Mama filling the gas tank once in a while.

Mama often put a kettle of sliced potatoes in water on the grate above one of the burners. The heat would cook the potatoes, which she then used to make bread.

On top of the refrigerator was a big sealed tank. I never knew what was in that tank. To satisfy my curiosity, I looked up gas refrigerators online. I read articles about how they worked, but I had a hard time understanding the process. I think the big tank held an ammonia solution.

Apparently the heat from the burners made ammonia gas produce bubbles which, after running through a system of tubes, somehow caused other things to happen, the result being that heat would be removed from the food storage area.

That old gas refrigerator, which dominated one corner of the kitchen, worked very well. I seem to remember it had a small section near the top for frozen food. We probably didn't need a big one anyway since Mama canned most of the foods we needed, including meats. If we wanted ice cream, we'd make a freezer full and eat it as soon as it was ready, allowing only a little time for it to set up just right.

If we were expecting company, there'd always be a bowl of Mama's favorite gelatin salad in the refrigerator. She made it by adding diced home-canned peaches, store-bought crushed pineapple, and grated carrots from the garden into orange-flavored gelatin. I loved that salad.

Mama usually cooked enough at noon so we could have leftovers for supper. The evening meal was then easy to prepare, just by getting cooked foods out of the refrigerator.

One of my favorite leftovers was cheese pockets, a German meal made by filling rolled-out dough Mama made which was similar to noodle dough. She cut it into squares and put on each square a spoonful of filling made of homemade dry cottage cheese flavored with onions. Then she folded the corners together and sealed the edges. At noon, we'd eat them with cream which had been fried down to pure butterfat with crackles in it. At night, we fried the pockets in butter. Yum! I won't even think about how many calories we consumed in one day!

In addition to keeping foods cold, the refrigerator provided a warm place to sit on cold days. I often pulled the rocker over close to it to read a book. Sometimes I looked up from my book to wonder why all that heat was making food cold. I don't think I understand it any better today than I did then.

Author and family posed in front of boxes of grapes on road trip to California. Left to right: Oscar Thum with author Marilyn in front, brother Marvin, mother Martha with sister Donna in front, sister Viona, cousin Bernetta Finck. Taken about 1949.

Road Trip

My parents, siblings, and I took only one real vacation in all my growing-up years, but it was a big one. Daddy sold a bull for $300 to get the money we'd need. He liked to joke, "We rode that bull all the way to California!" He figured that, when we got there, we'd stay in the homes of his cousins, whom we were going to visit. I often wonder how they felt about housing and feeding six of us for a few days.

Of course, we had to stay in motels on the three-day trips out and back. Those motels were nothing like the comfortable places we stay in these days. One had absolutely nothing but two or three beds in what looked like a wooden shack. Showers and toilets were located in another building. It was sort of like camping—only worse, because railroad tracks went right past our cabin. All night long, trains rattled by.

We usually got an early start in the mornings, eating meals along the way. We'd stop in a town and buy some bread, cold cuts, and maybe some fruit or cookies. Then Daddy would go to a cafe with our half-gallon canning jar and have it filled with coffee. We'd find some place along the road to have our "picnic."

Our relatives greeted us with enthusiasm I can only hope they felt. I know my dad was a favorite with them. He liked to joke and laugh. They made us feel at home—or maybe I was just too young to notice any grimaces as they prepared yet another meal for our family.

One evening, we were served hamburgers grilled outdoors—a first for our rural family. One of the women even had a nifty hamburger press. She'd put a fold of waxed paper with a ball of ground beef inside into the round wooden form, press down—and there was the patty ready for the grill. That impressed me!

Another time, the hostess served us shrimp cocktails. The little boiled shrimp were arranged around glasses of tangy sauce. We felt pretty "uptown" eating that!

One day, we were taken for a trip to Fisherman's Wharf. I don't remember much about that famous location, but I remember we ate at a restaurant which featured a large buffet. We'd never before seen anything like it. I chose, for my dessert, red Jell-O cut into little cubes. How gourmet was that!

As we moved from cousin to cousin, staying a few days with each, I looked forward to one particular experience. We'd been told that one of Daddy's cousins had a swimming pool on his farm. I'd never seen a private swimming pool. I imagined it would look like the ones Esther Williams enjoyed in movies I'd seen. But this was just a big square cement hole without even any water in it. I was very disappointed.

My daddy's cousins raised grapes on their farms. That seemed exotic to us coming from corn and oats country. We were intrigued by the Chinese workers who lived in small houses near the vineyards.

I have a lot of great memories from that wonderful vacation trip we took so many years ago. We had a great time, but I'm sure the best part was returning to good old South Dakota.

PRAIRIE ASTER

Laundry Day Back Then

I love to watch old movies on TV. Not only do they have great plots, but I know how everything in those movies worked. Still, however much I long for those simpler days, there's one day I'm glad I'm living in these modern times, and that's laundry day.

Mama selected me to be in charge of laundry when I was still a young girl. I didn't mind. I'm sure my sisters were kept busy doing other households jobs I'd rather not have done.

Daddy had hooked up our wringer washer to a motor. Either he or Mama filled the big metal tub of the machine with scalding hot water. Then I took over.

I grated part of a bar of Mama's homemade lye soap into the water and let it suds up while I sorted clothes. Since they'd all be washed in the same water, it was important to start with whites, then pastels, and gradually work my way through to darker colors. By that time, the water would have cooled off enough to keep them from fading.

After sloshing around in the washing machine for a few minutes, each load had to be run through the wringer attached to one side of the washtub and dropped into rinse water in a galvanized tub sitting beside the machine. I added a few drops of Mrs. Stewart's Bluing to the rinse water to be sure whites were sparkling white. Then the clothes had to be run back through the wringer onto the lid of the washing machine tub.

By that time, I had dissolved powdered starch in hot water. I'd dip shirts, blouses, and dresses into the mixture and wring them out by hand.

The next job was hanging clothes outside on lines to dry. In summer, clothes dried rapidly in the breeze. I remember my Uncle Art, who was often helping Daddy at our farm, teasing me that my washing was "tattletale gray," words in a popular detergent commercial of those days.

In winter, clothes froze on the line. Then they'd have to be brought in and hung around the kitchen to dry out.

Since we had no dryer to fluff clothes and permanent press synthetics weren't available to any great degree, most items we washed had to be ironed. That job was big enough to have a day of its own, as well as an entire essay written about it!

Looking back, I realize laundry day involved a lot of manual labor, but there were also those quiet moments while waiting for a load to finish washing. Maybe it was all the daydreaming I was able to do then that steered me into being a writer today. Since I enjoy writing, I am thankful I was the laundry girl at our house those many years ago.

Ironing Day Back Then

Ironing day was just that when I was a girl. It was a day when you spent most of the hours in it ironing. We hadn't even heard of permanent press or synthetics. Most clothing and linens were made of cotton, and they came off the wash lines stiff and wrinkled.

I remember folding a huge stack of dish towels Mama had made out of flour sacks to prepare them for ironing each week. I'd put the entire stack on the ironing board and iron and fold one at a time, exposing the towel beneath it. What a tedious job!

Dress clothes had to be sprinkled with warm water the evening before and wrapped in towels so they'd be a bit damp when ironing them. The glass sprinkler bottle had a long thin neck and a nozzle pierced with lots of little holes. I remember how wonderful we thought it was when plastic bags first became available. They kept sprinkled laundry just damp enough until we got to ironing it.

Our good dresses and Daddy's and my brother's shirts had been stiffened with starch before being sprinkled and ironed. Looking back, I realize all that work pressing them smooth lasted about five minutes after we put them on. I guess everyone walked around in wrinkled clothes those days.

The first irons we used were small and heavy. We heated several at a time on the cookstove top. The one detachable handle we had was inserted into the top of an iron when it was hot and ready to use. That meant the stove had to be hot to do the ironing, even on steaming summer days. No wonder they called them "sad irons."

Then Mama bought a gas iron. I'm not sure what kind of gas it burned in the small blue ball-shaped tank attached to its back. Mama had to use a little pump to force air into it every once in a while.

As soon as we obtained electricity on the farm, Mama bought an electric steam iron. No longer did we have to sprinkle clothes.

Daddy likely made the ironing board we used since it was entirely of wood. Mama padded the top with layers of old sheets pinned securely onto it.

I remember spending hours at the ironing board. Listening to soap operas on the radio helped keep my mind off the boring task. I still iron a few items in my laundry, but now I sit at an adjustable ironing board. I listen to the radio while I do it, just as I did when I was a girl, but nowadays, there are no soap operas being broadcast. I kinda miss them.

BACHELOR BUTTON

Author's grandmother Sophia Thum, at age 73. Taken in 1959.

The Portrait

Paint a halo of soft gray-brown braids around her head,

Braids she undid before bedtime to fall in springy waves

As she knelt to thank a benevolent God for daily blessings.

Add to her blue-gray eyes crinkly laugh lines radiating out

And a sparkle betraying a sense of humor

That sometimes enjoyed a touch of spice.

Add arthritic bumps to her small energetic hands,

And show them stirring a vat of golden chicken soup

Filled with thick noodles she made herself.

Across the back of her shoulders, add the hump

That grew bigger as she grew older,

A hump brought on by hauling baskets of laundry to the wash line

And stooping over to weed the garden she planted every spring.

Make her feet look as though she's hustling,

For she always had work to do and places to go
And people who needed her help and care.

Clothe her in a cotton housedress with an apron over it;

Be sure they reach a respectable length below her knees.

Then step back and see if you feel the love radiating out,

And, if you do, label the portrait with the name

By which she'd want to be remembered.

Call it "A Portrait of Grandma."

A Memorable Supper at Grandma's House

When we finally got electricity on the farm, a lot of wonderful new experiences came along with it. We loved having light at the flip of a switch. We looked forward to getting a television set as soon as they became efficient enough for people to enjoy. Mama treated us to T-bone steaks broiled in the oven of her new electric stove every Sunday noon. What a treat they were!

But one of the fondest memories I have of those times involved a newfangled appliance Grandma bought. She lived in town and had electricity all along. But she was a frugal woman, so she didn't buy unnecessary items. We were surprised and pleased when something prompted her to buy an electric waffle iron!

None of her grown children had such a modern device, so she decided to invite us to her house, one family at a time, for a Saturday night supper of crisp waffles and homemade pork sausage. We could hardly wait for our turn.

Of course, Grandma's house was a regular Saturday night stop. Before we went uptown to buy groceries, go to a movie, and visit with friends, we'd stop at Grandma's to deliver eggs, milk, cream, and other items we produced on the farm. The sausage she served with the waffles would have been some Mama and Daddy made themselves.

It was hard to wait for my turn as Grandma baked waffles as quickly as the shiny new waffle iron could make them. But they were worth the wait, topped with melting butter and syrup, with a chunk of sausage beside.

I suspect it took quite a while till our family had their fill since there were six of us, counting our parents. But I can still see Grandma smiling that perky smile of hers as she mixed the batter and cooked the sausage.

How we all loved our hardworking little Grandma with her wavy gray hair wound around her head and her knobby arthritic fingers always busy. Every visit to her house was enjoyable, but that night, when we came to eat waffles for the first time, is a visit I'll always remember and treasure.

Thanksgiving Appreciated

These days, as we gather for our Thanksgiving celebration, it's just a few adults around the table. How different from when I was a child, and both my grandmas' houses bustled with dozens of cousins as the extended family gathered to celebrate.

We always had two Thanksgiving dinners, one with each of my parents' families. One gathering was on Thanksgiving Day and one the next day. It couldn't get much better than that!

Since my mom's family was large, we had to eat in shifts. The men ate first, followed by the children. Then the women sat to the table for a leisurely meal and lots of talking and laughing.

We children were sent to the basement to play. If we got too loud, we would be allowed to go to the movie—which was our goal anyway. We must have made quite a sight as we entered the movie theater over twenty strong, older cousins with little ones in hand.

It was different at my paternal grandma's house. We could almost all fit around the table. Of course, the ladies held back to do the serving. I suspect they never did get any white meat from the turkey!

I don't suppose I fully appreciated the wonderful food those days. Most of the side dishes—mounds of creamy mashed potatoes, buttered corn and other vegetables, salads, pickled beets and cucumbers—would have been made from produce grown by my aunts.

My mom's specialty was nut pudding, a pure white concoction of chopped walnuts and whipped, sweetened vanilla-flavored cream from our own cows. Mama decorated the top with walnut halves and maraschino cherries.

After the meal, the aunts spent hours in the kitchen, washing dishes and cleaning up. They didn't mind. They enjoyed the chance to visit.

I'm thankful for those days when most extended families lived close enough to get together for the holidays. I grew up knowing my cousins, aunts, and uncles well. How I wish my own children had that advantage. We try to keep them close to the rest of the family with reunions every other year. But that can't compare to the richness of seeing all your relatives every holiday.

Next year, as I join the small group of adults at a quiet Thanksgiving meal, I'm going to give special thanks for those I experienced as a child. They were really something for which to be thankful.

My Mama's Nut Pudding

(This is a very rich side dish or a dessert.)

2 envelopes unflavored gelatin softened in ¼ cup cold water

2 eggs

1½ cups whole milk

¾ cup sugar

1½ cups whipping cream

1 tsp. vanilla

¾ cup chopped walnuts

Beat the eggs; add the sugar and milk. Put into top part of double boiler and cook until it comes to a boil and coats a spoon. Gradually stir egg mixture into softened gelatin until smooth. Cool, stirring occasionally.

Whip cream until stiff. Add vanilla. Stir into cooled egg mixture.

Stir walnuts into mixture. If desired, decorate top with walnut halves and maraschino cherries. Store in refrigerator.

PRAIRIE ASTER

Milking Cows: A Nasty Job— Especially on Saturday Afternoons

Before my dad finally installed milking machines in our barn, my siblings and I were expected to do the milking by hand, twice every day. It certainly wasn't my favorite job any time of the year.

It was bad enough on winter mornings when the barn was frigid and we had just barely enough light to see in the predawn hour. Then I didn't mind being close to the warm side of a cow. As she stood patiently in her stall, munching hay, I tried to absorb some of that warmth while I got on with the chore.

But milking in the summer was a different story, and doing it on Saturday afternoons was the worst!

To begin with, we'd wash our hair early Saturday morning and roll it up in pin curls held in place with bobby pins. We wanted curly hair for our trip to town on Saturday evening. We'd leave those pins in all day to be sure our hair was thoroughly dry before combing it into the style of the day.

Then came afternoon milking time. Our efforts at being in style barely survived.

First, because it was summer and flies were abundant in the barn, we'd have to spray the cows with horrible-smelling fly spray. I'm sure we wore "essence of fly spray" to town those Saturday evenings. But I guess everyone else did, too, so maybe nobody noticed.

Then, as we'd sit down on those precarious three-legged stools to milk, the cow would switch her tail to flick off flies that had withstood the spray. Of course, the cow's tail often got caught in our bobby pins. How I hated that. Sometimes I'd try to pinch the end of the cow's tail between my knee and the milk pail, but the cows didn't appreciate that very much.

By the time we were done milking, we were lucky to have any pins left in our hair. We'd have our bath and then take out the remaining pins. I suppose we felt the effort of pinning up our hair was worth the final result, in spite of the battle with the cows' tails. But the elimination of that battle was the main reason I was so happy when Daddy finally installed milking machines.

BLACK-EYED SUSAN

Author's father with his dog, Maddo.

A Trusting Friend

The farmer kneels beside the old dog,

Too choked with unshed tears to speak.

He lays his calloused hand on the shaggy brown head

As the years roll back to the day

He brought a playful pup to the farm.

From that time on, they'd been inseparable.

The dog understood the man's commands

And never failed to obey.

The man treasured the dog's faithfulness

Throughout long toil-filled days.

At sunset, they rested, side by side on the porch steps

In deep and silent companionship.

Now the dog, too frail to rise,

Looks up calmly into the man's eyes.

The man knows what must be done,

But he can't do it himself.

Early the next morning, his neighbor will come

To do the job, quickly and painlessly.

The man runs his hand gently down the dog's back one more time.

Then he stands and trudges to the house alone

While the dog watches with eyes full of love and trust.

He knows the man will do what must be done to end his pain.

He breathes a deep and contented breath and lays his tired head back down.

Catching Pullets

There was something special about summer evenings on the farm. The setting sun cast long shadows from the shelter belt over the yard, cooling it down from the scorching daytime heat. Dogs and cats napped on the front step, and even our mom and dad sat down and relaxed, perhaps for the first time all day.

Mama didn't make us wear our sunbonnets after supper, so we girls felt especially free to run and play. Sometimes we four siblings played hide-and-seek. That game was always a lot of fun when you had the entire farmyard for hiding places.

Or we'd play Ante Ante Over, throwing the baseball over a shed in the middle of the yard. I remember running and playing so hard that I couldn't seem to get enough water to quench my thirst and then ended up getting a water stomachache.

But, some early summer evenings, we had a chore to do that I really hated—catching pullets!

The tiny baby chicks Mama had bought in late winter grew up fast. When they were too big to stay in the small brooder house, they were allowed to run free all over the yard. By the time they were half grown, they had developed the habit of sleeping in low branches of trees in the shelter belt.

By then, the hens were called pullets and were about to begin laying eggs. Of course, we couldn't allow them to lay those eggs all over the farm, so we had to train them to sleep in the hen house where nests provided a convenient place for them to lay their eggs.

But first, we had to catch all those pullets sleeping in the trees and carry them down to the hen house to be locked in until they were used to living there.

How I hated reaching into the trees to catch those chickens. They scratched and flapped their wings and pecked at our arms. Feathers flew. Chickens squawked. And I'm sure we complained.

If the pullets were roosting too high in the tree, we had to use a pole with a strong wire hook at the end. We hooked their legs to pull them out of the tree.

By the time we had caught as many as we could—a few always escaped—we were dirty, sweaty, and a bit scratched up. But, after a few nights, the job was done, and we could gather eggs easily from nests in the hen house.

Of course, sometimes an old hen decided to lay a bunch of eggs somewhere outdoors. If she kept them hidden long enough, she eventually led a batch of fuzzy little chicks into the chicken yard. I loved that. And I don't suppose Mama was too upset about it either. It just added to her flock. I was happy that mother hen trained her chicks where to roost without any help from me!

PASQUE

Wild Plums, Chokecherries, and Other Treats from Long Ago

Wild plums and chokecherries were free for the picking when I was a girl. We'd gather buckets of them in ditches along country roads around our farmland. We'd also take home lots of mosquito bites and a few chiggers with our buckets of sun-ripened fruit, but we didn't complain. After all, it was for a good purpose.

Wild plum bushes were more plentiful and each plum was a lot larger than the small marble-sized chokecherries. As a result, Mama always made jars and jars of thick, red orange plum jam, but just a few jars of clear purple chokecherry jelly each summer.

I really got tired of the plentiful plum jam. We ate it on bread almost every day and mixed it into homemade cottage cheese. I was always relieved to see Mama open a jar of chokecherry jelly for a change. And having store-bought grape jelly was a real and rare treat.

It's been about fifty years since I ate plum jam, and you know what? I'd love a slice of Mama's home-baked bread slathered with a thick layer of plum jam right now!

I'd also love a bowl of fat juicy mulberries with sugar and ice-cold real cream on them. I'd even be willing to spread an old sheet under a mulberry tree as we used to do when I was a girl, to shake down the ripe berries—along with twigs, leaves, and spiders.

After sorting out the ripe berries from all the other stuff that had fallen onto the sheet, we had to snip the tiny stem from every berry before we could enjoy it. It was certainly a labor-intensive treat, but worth the effort.

You know what else I haven't eaten in a long time? Chicken feet! Yep, feet. Not drumsticks. Mama always fried the feet along with the rest of the spring rooster. She'd peel off the yellow outer skin to expose the tender white skin under it and snip off the claws. Then she'd dip the feet in flour and fry them up golden and crispy in lard. Of course, there wasn't much to eat on those little feet, which we always called "scratchers," but they surely were a tasty nibble.

One of these days real soon, I'm going to make a batch of peanut bars like Mama used to make. They're a fussy dessert requiring several steps, so Mama didn't make them often. I think I can use a few modern shortcuts. I'll include the recipe.

I'm not sure if the foods I remember from my childhood would taste as good to me now as they did back then, but they'd surely bring back lots of happy memories.

P e a n u t   C a k e   B a r s
(My Simple Version)

Bake one 9x13 yellow cake using your favorite recipe or a box mix. After cool, cut into 1-inch by 2-inch bars. Dip in thin powdered sugar icing (powdered sugar, melted butter, vanilla, milk). Then roll in finely crushed peanuts. Set on rack to dry.

BLACK-EYED SUSAN

Sweet Memories

They say smells trigger memories most vividly, but I think tastes are right up there with smells when it comes to remembering the past. Maybe it's because they're so closely related. And what tasted better than some of those great desserts we remember from our childhoods?

Just recently, when I bought the first really decent strawberries of the season, I remembered a wonderful strawberry chiffon pie my mom used to make. Unfortunately, I can't find her recipe for it.

This wonderful pie always started with a trip to my Aunt Viola and Uncle Art's farm because Viola had a big strawberry patch in her garden. When the berries were ripe, she asked us to help pick them. Our reward would be a big bucket of them to take home.

I'm sure we took a lot of them home in our stomachs, too. What is more delicious than a vine-ripened strawberry, still warm from the sun? They were so different from those we buy in the store nowadays.

For one thing, they weren't as big as they are now. But they were much softer and juicier and sweeter. And they were actually red all the way through. When you hulled and sliced those strawberries and sugared them down, they formed a wonderful strawberry syrup, right there in the bowl. Nothing ever tasted better served over homemade vanilla ice cream.

Or a piece of homemade angel food cake. It seems to me all the ladies tried to outdo each other with the highest and fluffiest angel food cake. One of our neighbor ladies was well known for her tall, snowy-white angel food cakes. I remember my mom saying she suspected that lady added an extra egg white or two to the recipe.

A dessert I made often as a girl was a rich devil's food cake. It needed one cup of thick sour cream straight from the cream can in the basement to which we had added each day's cream after separating it from the skim milk. That cream soured naturally into a smooth mass so thick you could stand a spoon up in it.

I still have that cake recipe, written in my childish handwriting in an old notebook, but I can no longer make it because I can't find a suitable substitute for the sour cream. I've tried commercial sour cream, whipping cream, buttermilk, a combination of cream and butter, but nothing works. That's one recipe that will have to live on only as a memory.

My grandma was famous for a yellow cake she made. Its broiled coconut icing complemented the soft moist cake. It was always called "Reiger Cake" because the recipe came from the wife of our Pastor Reiger.

I'm going to dig out that old recipe notebook and see what other memory-inducing sweets I find. I probably won't make them because these days we try to limit our intake of sweets, but that won't stop me from wallowing in wonderful memories connected to them.

Marilyn's Red Devil's Food Cake

(This cake has my name beside it in Mama's recipe notebook because I made it so often, but not anymore! I just can't find a proper substitute for the sour cream I used from the cream can in the basement of our farm home. It was nothing like the cultured sour cream we buy these days. I always topped this cake off with fluffy, cooked, brown sugar and egg whites icing. Then I grated unsweetened chocolate over the top. Yummy!)

2 eggs

1 cup thick sour cream

1 cup white sugar

1 teaspoon vanilla

1 teaspoon baking soda

1¼ cup all purpose flour

3 tablespoons unsweetened cocoa powder

¼ teaspoon salt

Sift dry ingredients together. Beat eggs well. Add sour cream and sugar to eggs. Add egg mixture to dry ingredients. Mix well. Pour into well-greased 9x13 or two round 8- or 9-inch cake pans. Bake in 350 degree oven for 30-35 minutes.

In the Good Old (Un-Air-Conditioned) Summertime

Do you ever wonder how we survived in the days before every house, store, and car was equipped with frigid air conditioning? I don't remember feeling as hot back then as I would now if my AC quit on an eighty-plus degree day. I'm sure it had a lot to do with not knowing anything different. But maybe our coping strategies were what made those long-ago hot and humid days bearable.

It helped to be living in the country with no close buildings to block the available breezes. The shelter belt, on the north and west sides of the farmyard, kept away only cold winter winds. Those tall, dense elms provided cool shade for the house starting about midafternoon each day.

Most farmhouses had two stories. That helped keep the downstairs cool. The upstairs, where we slept, didn't cool off much at night.

Often my sisters and I would leave our bedroom with its one west window and sneak into our brother's room where we could feel a breeze coming in his south or east windows. It also felt cooler to sleep on a blanket on the floor instead of sinking into the puffy homemade feather-filled mattresses on our beds.

Mama had ways to help us keep cool, too. She'd fill a glass milk bottle with a combination of fresh milk and instant Postum drink. How cooling and refreshing that tasted as we passed the bottle around on hot summer afternoons.

Somehow, eating a dill pickle straight from the crock in the cellar seemed to have a cooling effect, too. Those pickles tasted especially good with a slice of Mama's homemade bread, slathered with fresh butter and plum jelly. How "cool" is that!

Sometimes, my younger sister and I cooled off by plunging our arms into the water in the big stock tanks. The windmill nearby filled the tanks with refreshingly cold well water. If our parents left us home alone on a hot summer day, my siblings and I would "swim" in the tanks. We had no idea how dangerous that could be. We apparently didn't think about the mouths of the cows and horses which had slobbered in the water. We also ignored the mossy, slimy tank walls and bottom. We just wanted to cool off.

I recall one afternoon when we almost got caught "swimming." Our underwear, which served as our swimwear, was still drying on the wash line that day when our uncle came to check something on the threshing machine he owned with Dad. I don't know if he noticed the evidence of our swim on the wash line, but he probably saw the guilty looks on our faces. He didn't say anything to our parents—as far as I know.

These days, we don't tolerate heat as well as we did years ago. We just depend on our air conditioners to take care of us. I must admit, I'm thankful for mine. I doubt that a dill pickle and jelly bread sandwich would cool me off in my modern one-story ranch-style house these days. They probably wouldn't even taste the same as they did back then when that was one way to beat the heat.

Dill Pickles

(Mama marked these pickles "very good" in her old recipe notebook. She also added a note that says she received this recipe from her mother-in-law in 1948. Mama loved to eat pickles when they were just beginning to turn sour.)

1 gallon water

1 cup vinegar

1 cup canning/pickling salt

1 tablespoon alum

1 tablespoon pickling spice

Pack pickles in about eight quart jars with fresh dill on top and bottom. Bring brine ingredients to a boil. Pour over pickles and dill. Seal.

You could check cookbooks to see how to seal them. Mama used lids that needed a red rubber ring inside to make a seal. If two-part lids are used, the jars can be set into a canner and covered with at least one inch of cold water. Bring slowly to a boil. Turn off heat and let jars sit in water until cool and lids pop to indicate seal.

Our Fresh Air Taxi and Other Unusual Playthings on the Farm

Farm machines were sometimes our source of entertainment when my siblings and I were children. I suspect we occasionally took risks our parents would not have wanted us to take, but we were never bored.

I loved watching Daddy move hay up into the loft at the top of the barn. He used a system of ropes laid on the hayrack before hay was loaded onto it. When he pulled on the ropes using his horses and, later, a tractor, the ropes swooped up on each side of the hay until they came together at the top of the pile. Then they lifted the huge bundle of hay to the open hayloft door. Next we'd hear a loud click, and the hay would shoot into the barn on pulleys riding along a track in the peak of the roof.

The threshing machine, feed grinder, and corn auger were fascinating to us, too, but we knew we had to stay back from them when they were in use. That didn't stop us from playing around on machines that were just sitting there, enticing us.

My little sister and I often played with the hay rake. It had a long row of big curved iron teeth which raked the hay into furrows. We'd stick clumps of grass into the little spaces where the teeth were connected to the machine. Then we'd push the teeth back and forth to grind up the grass. I don't suppose Daddy appreciated the mess we made.Along the back of Daddy's partially underground shop was a pile of scrap iron. We found all sorts of things to play with there. We helped ourselves to odds and ends from that pile to make our "houses" in the shelter belt.

Sitting under a big elm tree in a far corner of the yard was an old buggy with a wooden seat. I don't remember ever seeing it hitched up to a horse. In fact, I don't think it was ever moved from its resting spot. On one side of it, someone had painted the words "Fresh Air Taxi." My siblings and I took many a fanciful trip in that buggy. The long wooden tongue extending from its front made a perfect balance beam for us.

Sometimes we climbed up a few steps on the big windmill beside the barn. I don't remember ever climbing all the way to the top. I suspect we were tempted to try, but apparently our parents' warnings against that adventure kept us grounded.

We always found something to do on the farm. If all else failed, there were the stock tanks. But that's another story—one I've already told!

PRAIRIE ASTER

Farmers unload oats bundles into threshing machine. Oats kernels drop into wagon while straw shoots out at back of the machine. Photo used with permission of Bonita Davison.

Threshing Day— Fun for a Child

Threshing day was filled with fun for me when I was a little girl. The excitement actually began the day before when my great-uncle brought his big dinosaur-looking threshing machine to our farm. Daddy helped him set it up and level it in the pasture where he wanted the straw stack to sit. If the wind changed the next morning, they'd have to move it so that chaff created by the threshing process blew away from the men unloading bundles into it. We children were warned not to go near it, but we could look.

Early the next morning, I watched teams of horses gather in our yard. Neighbors and relatives joined to thresh Daddy's oats crop just as they would on their own farms, one after another, until all were done. It was such a big job that it had to be shared.

The teams pulled big hayracks across the field where my sister and I had shocked the grain. As the summer sun beat down on them, the men tossed oats-laden bundles onto the racks using pitchforks.

One by one, the loaded racks were drawn up beside the threshing machine. The men pitched bundles into the machine, which then separated oats kernels from stems of straw. The threshing machine was powered by a wide belt and pulley connected to the tractor. All day long, the sound of the tractor's motor echoed across the yard.

As the day wore on, the men became hotter and grimier. My brother remembers feeling sorry for the horses when he saw their heads droop in weariness.

The men and their horses weren't the only ones working hard. It was a busy day for Mama, too.

She'd be up early preparing food for midmorning and afternoon "lunches," as well as a big midday dinner. I remember hearing her ask Dad what he'd been served at the other farms so she could make something different.

Lunches consisted of sandwiches and homemade cookies, kuchen or kolaches, along with a big blue-enameled pot of hot coffee. Mama set it up in a shady spot, often in the shadow cast by the big tractor wheel where a cream can of water sat all day long. The men came, one or two at a time, to eat. I always went out with Mama so I could get a closer look at all the excitement.

At noon, the men stopped working long enough to eat dinner. Mama set up a washstand on the north side of the house so the dusty men could clean up. Then they all gathered around the kitchen table where Mama served platters of fried chicken or roast beef, mounds of mashed potatoes, side dishes, and often pie for dessert.

I loved listening to the men laugh and talk while they ate. They had some fun on threshing day, too. The hard work didn't get them down. That's the way farmers were back then, and still are.

A team of horses similar to those owned by author's father. Photo used with permission of Loretta Sorensen.

DollarBill

Their names were Dolly and Bill, Dad's team of sturdy farm horses,

But he called them DollarBill just to make us laugh.

To my childhood eyes, they looked immense

As they stood patiently in their stalls,

Waiting to be led out for the day's work.

Their rich sorrel color set off their soft blond manes and tails.

They stamped their frypan-sized hooves to chase off flies

And chuffed as they munched their oats.

Dad's pride in them was evident in the way

He showed respect for them.

He spoke softly when he approached their stall,

Their heavy leather harnesses draped over his back.

Dad curried them to keep their coats shining and comfortable,

Especially after a day of pulling the hayrack in hot summer sun

While he filled it to overflowing with shocks of golden-ripe oats.

Each day before he left the barn,

He checked their heavy hooves

To be sure no imbedded rocks brought pain to their steps.

He kept his horses around even after tractors

Took over jobs they used to do,

But the day came when he had to sell them.

He didn't talk as he led them up the ramp, into the truck box,

And ran his hands one more time over their broad sides.

He didn't watch the truck drive down the lane

And out to the graveled road, taking them away.

I doubt he ever stopped missing them.

Saturday Night in Town

Saturday night in town when I was a girl actually started early Saturday morning. Mama would mix up a big batch of dough so, later, we could have a quick supper of caramel rolls and cold fried chicken or sliced ham. We didn't want to do a big pile of supper dishes.

Then Mama, my sisters, and I would wash our hair and roll it up in pin curls. We'd walk around like that all day while our hair dried. How we complained when the cows' switching tails caught in the bobby pins as we did the late afternoon milking. We all had a weekly bath after supper, changed into "almost Sunday" clothes, and headed off to town.

Our first stop was at the creamery to drop off the five-gallon can of thick sour cream. All week long it had sat in the basement as we added each day's cream after separating it from the skim milk.

The second stop was at the back of the grocery store to unload a case or two of eggs gathered during the week. The egg check paid for the groceries Mama bought. I remember standing beside Mama, when I was very young, as she read her list to the clerk. That energetic person hurried about, gathering the items. I wasn't much older when shopping carts finally arrived, making the job of shopping easier for all concerned.

Mama finished her grocery shopping early in the evening. Items needing refrigeration were labeled with her name and placed in the cooler alongside the food offered for sale. The rest of the groceries were packed into our emptied egg cases. These were set along the outside walls of the store along with those of all the other farm customers. There they'd stay all evening. It amazes me now how trustworthy everyone was. I don't ever recall an item being stolen from our boxes.

After the grocery shopping was done and any other needed purchases were made, Mama would join friends and relatives sitting in cars parked along Main Street for an evening of visiting. The men clustered on the corner near the bars.

We children went to the movie—usually a Western. It cost nine cents. That left a nickel of my fifteen cents allowance for a treat (does anyone make chocolate root beer floats anymore?) and a penny left for collection at church the next day. We had time after the movie to walk up and down the street, window-shopping and having fun with our friends.

About ten or ten thirty, we'd all head for the car. We'd pick up our groceries, the empty cream can, and the cream check. Then we'd stop for a double-dip ice cream cone for everyone in the family.

Our last stop would be at the gas station, where Daddy would get one dollar's worth of gas—which lasted all week.

As we headed for home, we were already anticipating next Saturday night in town.

BACHELOR BUTTON

Our Heroes

When we were kids, the cowboys' lives

Seemed filled with song and glory

Because the only ones we knew

Were in a movie story.

Each Saturday we went to town

And headed for the show.

We waited for the lights to dim

And for the screen to glow.

Then there were Roy and Dale and crew

And Trigger, Roy's great horse.

And bad men wearing tall black hats,

And Gabby Hayes, of course.

Or it might be my brother's choice—
Gene Autry with his songs.
His horse named Champion and his pal
Pat Buttram came along.

It didn't make a difference

Which hero's film we saw.

We knew the good guys always won;

That was the cowboy law.

BLACK-EYED SUSAN

Entrance to rural school author attended with artwork in windows.
Taken in the late 1940s.

Art in a Rural School

We loved "art class" in the little one-room rural school I attended. It always came during the last period on Fridays. Usually the teacher had copies of seasonal pictures for the younger students to color. While that may not have been especially creative, they seemed to enjoy it, and it kept them busy. The older students would have more interesting projects, although I think they were more in the line of crafts than art.

I remember one time when we were shown how to make a 3-D sunflower. We started by folding yellow construction paper petals in half. Then we glued down one half of each petal around a brown circle on a piece of white paper. The other half stuck up, making it look like a real flower. We added stem, leaves, and background. I was so proud of my sunflower masterpiece that I kept it for years.

The teacher displayed our artworks by taping them in the windows or tacking them up along the bottom of the chalk rail under the blackboard. We loved seeing our art around the room.

In the school basement, we had a workbench with a few tools. Sometimes we'd make small wooden items to give our parents as gifts. I can't remember what I made, but I do remember I used a small can of paint labeled "apple green" for some of my projects.

When I wasn't in classes or studying, I spent a lot of time drawing pictures on the back of corrected assignment papers. I was always happy when the assignment left the entire back of the paper free for me to draw rainbow scenes, princesses, or flowers.

About once every six weeks, we had "picture study" using a booklet which contained pictures of famous paintings and information about the artists. After the study, we each received a little sticker with the painting reproduced on it. How I wish I had saved those beautiful little stickers.

We had four major works of art on display on the walls of our schoolroom. At front were Gilbert Stuart's painting of George Washington and a portrait of Abraham Lincoln based on a photograph by Matthew Brady. Along a side wall were Rose Bonheur's *Horse Fair* and a painting of a huge sailing ship named *Old Ironsides*. I can still see those paintings in my mind's eye.

I don't suppose any of us children had ever been to an art gallery, but we liked pretty pictures, whether our own or those in books. And when we wanted to see a beautiful landscape, all we had to do was look around at the farms and meadows surrounding us. They are still my favorite works of art.

A Different Kind
of Halloween

Can you imagine Halloween without trick-or-treating? When I was a girl growing up in a rural area over sixty years ago, trick-or-treating wasn't part of Halloween for me or my friends. That doesn't mean we felt left out of that holiday celebration. On the contrary, we spent weeks preparing for it in the one-room country school I attended.

About a month before October 31, the boys and girls in the upper grades began to plan—seriously and secretly. Decorations had to be designed, food had to be solicited from moms, and disgusting tricks had to be arranged to horrify the littlest children. Getting to be big enough to be part of that delightful, secret planning was a major goal of my first years in school.

About a week before Halloween Day, the basement of our school building became off-limits for anyone not in on the preparations. Corn shocks from the field beside our playground were hauled down and set around the room. Considering the basement housed a coal-burning furnace, that was certainly a scary idea. It amazes me now that the school board wasn't worried enough about fire to forbid the corn shocks, but they never did. The carved pumpkins with real candles burning inside didn't seem to bother them either. Apparently, they trusted us to be careful.

Black and orange crepe paper streamers festooned the entire ceiling downstairs. Pictures of jack-o'-lanterns, witches, ghosts, and bats which the little children had colored were taped to the walls. The windows were covered over with paper so the room would be suitably dark and spooky.

Our teacher allowed us to have an entire afternoon for the party. Part of that time was needed for donning our costumes. For weeks, we had planned just what we would be. Our parents couldn't afford store-bought costumes, so we had to make them ourselves using whatever we could find. We usually spent part of our meager allowances on masks since homemade masks didn't hold up very well.

Games included blindfolding the little children and making them feel eyeballs (grapes), intestines (cooked spaghetti), and other gross items. We always had a big galvanized tub of water to bob for apples, an activity I hated. Maybe that's because I never could get an apple.

The last event of the afternoon was the lunch provided by some of the moms. We stuffed ourselves on orange-frosted cupcakes and cookies, orange drinks, candy corn, and popcorn balls.

I suppose we'd heard about trick-or-treating in those days, but, after our half-day party at school, we were satisfied that we'd celebrated Halloween about as well as it could be celebrated. My memories of those special days bring back feelings of joy—even though I still prefer getting my apples from my tree or the store.

PASQUE

Grandma's Summer Kitchen

My three siblings and I were between the ages of about two to eight when our mother had to be hospitalized for a couple of weeks. Mama's parents took care of us at our home for the first week. Then they had to get back to their farm. They left reluctantly, leaving Daddy to look after us by himself.

Daddy needed help. He wasn't one to do housework or cooking, let alone take care of us and all his outside chores. So he asked his mom to let us stay with her for a while.

Grandma lived on a farm a few miles from ours. Back then, her two youngest sons were still at home. We loved Grandma and were happy to be staying with her and our jolly young uncles, both in their early twenties.

Besides that, Grandma had something on her farm we didn't have—a summer kitchen—a building sitting just beside the main house.

The main house was an old sod building with foot-thick walls and low ceilings. Its windows were small, and the kitchen was long and narrow, so it held the heat from cooking.

That's why Grandma cooked and did her canning in the summer kitchen on hot days. It was actually a two-room frame building with wide windows and a large kitchen. The other room was a combination bed/sitting room.

That other room had a big attraction for us children. Hanging on the west wall was a big, dark brown, wooden box with a bed inside. At night, Grandma would unfold the box from the wall, prop its bottom end up on foldaway legs, and there was our bed. We thought that was pretty neat!

I hope we didn't make too much extra work for Grandma all those days we had to stay with her. I think we were four pretty well-behaved children.

My older sister remembers once hiding behind Grandma's sauerkraut crock in a corner of the kitchen when she'd done something that sent Grandma after her. My Uncle Bob told me years later that he did have to spank me once. I'm not sure what I did to deserve it, and he's been gone a few years now, so that will remain a mystery.

I do remember one time we all got into trouble at Grandma's. She'd given us fresh oranges for a snack. Somehow we got the idea of punching holes in the oranges and then pushing them, with our mouths over the holes, against the thick round bar which was the handle on her oven door. By squishing the oranges up and down on the bar, we could squeeze juice into our mouths. Grandma didn't like the mess that made.

Both the houses on Grandma's farm are long gone. But I'll always have happy memories of time spent in them, especially that summer kitchen.

PRAIRIE ASTER

Eating Popcorn
Isn't What It Used to Be

There's something so cozy about a winter evening with a bowl of hot buttered popcorn to munch. And how easy it is these days to pop a bag into the microwave and have that treat ready to eat in a minute or two. But, you know what? I don't think it tastes nearly as good as the popcorn we ate years ago when making it was a whole lot harder.

First, we had to shell the corn off those little cobs. I don't remember if my dad raised popcorn in his fields; it may have come from my grandparents who raised many different crops on their farm. But I do remember shelling it. Those kernels had sharp, pointy little tips that liked to dig into our fingers as we worked.

Then we had to be sure the old iron cookstove in the kitchen was really hot. That meant filling the firebox with lots of dry cobs we'd carried in earlier, and adding more and more as the popcorn popped.

To pop the corn, we used a wire mesh basket with a lid of the same material and a long handle. We'd pour in the little white corn kernels, secure the lid tightly with a wire hook, and start shaking the basket directly on the hot stove top. Since there were six in our family, we usually made more than one wire basket full.

Mama would put the fluffy hot kernels into the big pan we used to wash dishes (no sink back in those days) and pour over them lots of home-churned butter that had been melting at the back of the stove. We didn't spare the salt either. We weren't worried so much about cholesterol and high blood pressure those days.

We'd all pull our chairs up to the kitchen table with the pan of hot popcorn in the middle, and we'd dig in. We were always careful not to bite into the unpopped kernels we called "old maids" which settled to the bottom of the pan.

Now here's the best part. We didn't watch television in silence as we snacked on popcorn. Of course, we didn't have a television set back then. So we talked to each other all the while. Imagine that!

While I'd be the first to admit it's much easier to enjoy popcorn these days, I'd also insist it isn't the same treat it used to be back then when it was harder to make and more "social" to eat.

Popcorn Balls

(Mama often made popcorn balls around Christmastime. We considered them a real treat. I found several recipes for them in her old cookbooks. This one seemed the easiest to make, although I haven't tried it.)

2 cups white sugar

½ cup white corn syrup

1 tablespoon vinegar

1¼ cups water

Butter the sides of a heavy pan and put the ingredients listed in it. Boil this mixture until it spins a thread (to about 250 degrees on a candy thermometer). It takes about 20-25 minutes.

Remove from heat and add:

1 teaspoon vanilla

½ teaspoon salt

Pour over about 15–18 cups popped corn in a buttered pan. Stir quickly until the popcorn is coated. Let cool a few minutes. Butter your hands and form the mixture in baseball-sized balls. Wrap in waxed paper.

BACHELOR BUTTON

Butchering Day

I don't remember butchering day with the details Laura Ingalls Wilder included in her delightful *Little House in the Big Woods* book. I would have been in school when my parents butchered since it was done late in fall when the weather was cold enough to freeze meat outdoors. But I do remember some of the work that went on afterwards as the meat was being processed.

One of the biggest jobs was making sausage. My parents made a mixture of pork and beef. After the meat was ground and seasoned to their taste, they packed it into the sausage-stuffing machine. The casings they used curled into big loops as the meat mixture was squeezed into them. That was fun to watch. Next the sausage was smoked in a smokehouse right on the farm.

Mama canned a lot of meat because we had no freezer. That meat tasted wonderful, having been cooked in its own juices.

Every part of the critter was used. I liked sausage and all the meat we had to eat, but there was one dish Mama made that I refused to touch: pork brains scrambled with eggs and onions. It may have tasted great—I'll never know—but it looked terrible.

Mama used all the meat she could find on the head and neck of the hog to make "headcheese." She boiled the bits of meat with seasonings for a long time. Then she'd chill it until it set up with the consistency of Jell-O. It made a good breakfast sandwich when sliced.

Recently I ran across something that brought back another memory of butchering day. It's Mama's recipe for homemade lye soap. She made soap every time we butchered. It was the only soap she used for laundry, and it did a great job.

Before she could start making soap, she rendered pieces of raw fat in a big kettle. That took a long time because she had to keep the heat fairly low. Finally, the kettle would contain liquid lard and crisp brown cracklings.

There are recipes that call for cracklings, but Mama never used them to cook. She saved them for our cats and dogs to eat. She was careful to dole them out a little at a time so the animals wouldn't overeat and get sick. The rich cracklings made their coats extra thick and shiny.

Mama used lard along with lye, Borax, grated Ivory soap bars, and Chipso (a laundry detergent available back then) in her recipe. After she stirred it all together, she poured the very thick mixture into big, flat cardboard boxes and set it aside to harden. Then she cut it into bars using a big butcher knife. I remember seeing her do that. It wasn't easy because the soap set up into a hard slab.

I can still remember the scent of Mama's lye soap. It smelled fresh and clean.

Butchering and processing meat were big jobs for people years ago. But the results were worth the effort.

Good White Soap

(Mama got this recipe from my dad's mom. I remember Mama using Rinso detergent instead of Chipso sometimes. She said it made the soap smell good.)

2½ gallons water

2 gallons melted lard

4 cans lye

1 box Borax

1 large package Chipso detergent

1 large bar Ivory soap

Take 1½ gallons of cold water and pour over lye in large bucket. Pour 1 gallon of boiling water over Chipso and grated Ivory soap in large bowl. Cool until lukewarm. Then add to lard. Add lye water which has been heated to lukewarm. Stir well, and add Borax last. Stir until it thickens. Pour into paper boxes to the depth of about 2 inches. Let set until hard enough to slice into bars.

BLACK-EYED SUSAN

Author's childhood farm home during winter of 1974-75.

You Think This Is Cold?

It's easy to complain about cold and snow even though most of us have no trouble keeping warm in our well-heated homes and cars. But do we appreciate how lucky we are these days? Maybe a look back to when we were children might remind us how easy we really have it now.

When we went to bed on a cold winter night, we might feel a bit of warmth still radiating up to our bedroom from the iron cookstove, fired up with corncobs, in the kitchen just below us. But that fire died down long before the night was over. I don't think we even noticed the cold creeping into the room as we snuggled deep into our feather beds.

Mama told me the water in the teakettle she kept on the stove was often frozen when she got up in the morning. She hurried to get the fire going in the cookstove to make the breakfast coffee and warm up the kitchen. The heat didn't make its way fast enough up through the register in the kitchen ceiling to us children to warm us while we dressed, so we often grabbed our clothes and ran down the stairs to dress in front of the open oven door.

Of course, that necessary Saturday night bath had to be taken with the big galvanized tub sitting close to the stove. I'm sure we shivered the minute we stepped out of the warm water because the stove couldn't heat the entire kitchen very well. Think about that the next time you step out of a steaming shower which has warmed your small bathroom into a sauna!

Mama kept the washstand out in the unheated front porch as long as weather allowed. Then she moved the small wooden stand with its white enameled pitcher of water and matching washbasin into the kitchen. Beside it she sat what was always called the "slop pail." That's where we emptied the dirty water after washing up.

Remember the days when the wash froze solid on the lines and had to be hung around the kitchen to dry?

Or plowing through snow to an unheated barn where you welcomed the warmth of the cow's body as you tried to get your frozen fingers moving well enough to do the milking?

Now, if all that hasn't made you stop complaining about cold winter weather, all I need mention is "outhouse." Had enough?

Even though we certainly weren't as comfortable in cold weather back then as we are now, we didn't know anything different, so we didn't complain. I guess it's really a good thing we live in the present and can't remember every detail of the past or look into the future.

My First Grown-up Christmas Dress

When I was about ten years old, I thought the one thing that would make me feel really grown up would be to have a Christmas dress that wasn't red or trimmed with lace, as all my Christmas dresses up to that time seemed to have been.

Mama made all our dresses, so that year I put in a request for a brown corduroy skirt with a matching brown, green, and cream checks. I'd wear it with a cream-colored blouse. I suppose I had seen a picture of such an outfit in a catalog.

Mama found just the perfect fabrics in town and set about sewing the outfit. I'm sure she made the pattern herself, as she usually did. And I'm sure she bought just the bare minimum amount of fabric so it wouldn't cost too much. She did allow enough so I could have a big box pleat down the front of the skirt, folding over the front seam.

I felt very grown up when I tried on the finished outfit and viewed myself in the mirror. Then I noticed something was wrong with the skirt. It looked like two different shades of brown. I brushed my hands down the front of the skirt and realized Mama had sewn the two front panels together with the nap of the corduroy going in opposite directions.

Now maybe it was Mama's first experience with corduroy. Or maybe she hadn't bought enough fabric to make the nap run the same way on both front pieces. I'll never know. But I was heartsick to see the result. I'm sure Mama noticed it, too, but she didn't say anything. Maybe she thought I hadn't noticed and didn't want to upset me by mentioning it.

I knew I couldn't ask Mama to make the skirt over. There was no fabric left, nor would she have had time. I had to wear it as it was if I wanted to have a new outfit for Christmas.

The first occasion to which I would wear the outfit was our Christmas program in the rural school I attended. I didn't think people would notice my two-shades skirt for most of the program because I'd be on stage with lots of other children.

But I wouldn't be able to hide it when my classmate Myrna and I were on stage alone, singing "Silent Night" in two-part harmony. We'd practiced so hard, and I'd looked so forward to this shining moment. But I couldn't help feeling embarrassed as I stood there on stage with my two-tone skirt.

The teacher started playing the piano. Myrna and I began singing. I looked over the heads of the parents sitting in front of us on planks supported by nail kegs in that little one-room school. I felt my cheeks turn red. Then I glanced down at Mama. She was gazing up at me with a look of love and pride, her face beaming.

That's when I realized that what I was wearing wasn't nearly as important as the love Mama showed me when she worked so hard to make my special Christmas outfit. I lifted my eyes and sang with all my heart. I felt confident and beautiful.

And I know I grew up just a little bit.

PASQUE

Christmas Meals at Grandma's House

The country school Christmas program wasn't the only one we had to get ready for when we were young. Our Sunday School classes at the church we attended in town also prepared a presentation to be given on Christmas Eve.

We practiced on Sunday afternoons so farm families wouldn't have to drive into town an extra time. That meant we got to have dinner at my *Klein* Grandma's house in town, something I always enjoyed. (*Klein* is the German word for little; she was only about five feet tall.)

Grandma knew how to make the best chicken noodle soup, which is what she served before the meat and potatoes part of the dinner. Her soup was rich with noodles she made herself, cut very thin. It took me years to learn how to make a broth almost as tasty as hers. Her secret may have been that she didn't strain off the layer of chicken fat on top, something we do in these cholesterol-conscious days.

Since all of Grandma's children lived on farms, she had a good supply of meat and dairy products donated by them to cook up for us to enjoy. While I'm sure the main part of the meal was delicious, her desserts made the next most lasting impression after the soup. It might be pie or cake, but it was always wonderful.

Sometimes she served us her unbeatable sour cream cookies with brown sugar icing. They looked like little flying saucers—actually not so little. Each cookie was about four inches across, and every bite was heavenly. I have the recipe, but, when I make them now, they simply don't taste as good. I guess I just don't have my grandma's touch.

We all gathered at Grandma's house again on December 26 (called Second Christmas Day back then) for a holiday party. At that event, she didn't provide a meal. Instead, we had finger foods served off the big table in her dining room. All the aunts brought food to share, but Grandma made a lot of it. No one could make caramels as delicious as hers. She made one other holiday treat which I still miss—homemade root beer. The stuff we get in bottles and cans these days just can't hold a candle to the bright-tasting drink Grandma made. It was the perfect accompaniment to holiday cookies, candies, and nuts.

Klein Grandma was a special person in so many ways. She loved being with people and helping them. She loved to laugh and always had a twinkle in her eye. But most of all she loved to see people enjoy her cooking. And I did.

As Christmas comes each year, I think back to those happy times in Grandma's dining room with its lace-curtained windows and old-fashioned furniture. Sometimes, I can almost smell the chicken noodle soup.

PRAIRIE ASTER

A Christmas Memory

I spent much of that Christmas Eve afternoon, so many years ago, looking out the window, waiting to see my sister Vi's car approach. She had moved in with Grandma in town earlier that year to be near her job, and I missed having her at home on the farm. What a Christmas we would have! Vi had hinted about the gifts she'd be bringing, thanks to having a paycheck of her own.

At last the car came up the lane and stopped at the house. With much laughter and talking, my parents, sister, brother, and I helped Vi unload the many boxes she'd brought. I could hardly wait for Mama to say, "Let's open presents."

But it was Vi who spoke of them first.

"Before we open our gifts, we must visit Lena," she said.

I knew our neighbor lady Lena was terminally ill with cancer. The last thing I wanted to do on that joyous day was spend time with her and her family.

I tried to hide my disappointment as I helped Vi and Mama fix a basket of fruit to take along. I hoped the visit would be short.

Lena's husband and two teenaged sons greeted us with sad eyes. They led us into the living room of their farmhouse where Lena sat on the couch, propped up with pillows.

At first, everyone spoke quietly and in a guarded way. But soon, thanks to Lena's courageous smile and ready laugh, we were visiting just as we always had.

When we left, I could see a lift to Lena's family's spirits. Perhaps our visit showed them that, even though they knew this would be Lena's last Christmas, they could count on their friends and neighbors to be there to help them through difficult days to come.

When we got home and began to open our gifts, I think we all felt the visit had made our Christmas richer. Giving of ourselves helped us enjoy our gifts in a new, more profound way.

I know I had often heard the Bible quotation, "It is more blessed to give than receive," before that day and have heard it many times since. But I'll always be thankful to my dear sister Vi for showing me what that saying means in a very special way so many years ago.

My Childhood Christmas Tree

I've never liked artificial Christmas trees. Oh, I know they're much easier to handle and cheaper in the long run since you can use them over and over, but they just don't seem right to me. For one thing, they don't have that woodsy, spicy smell of a real fir tree. And for another, they're too perfect. Lopsided means real in my book.

So it's strange that the tree I remember most from my childhood was actually an artificial tree. That little "bottlebrush" tree has lingered in my memory longer and more firmly than any of the tall and beautiful real trees we decorated when our children were still at home.

It wasn't very big, probably only about eighteen inches high, and it had very few branches. They really did look like long green brushes. It was anchored in a small red pot filled with plaster of Paris. I don't know where Mama bought it. Maybe she ordered it from a catalog.

We had no store-bought decorations for the tree. We made our own. We started with a string of popcorn and sometimes a raw cranberry string to wind around the branches. For something sparkly, we'd glue string loops to empty walnut shells and wrap the shells tightly in discarded pieces of tinfoil.

One of my favorite homemade decorations started with regular-sized marshmallows. We'd make red dots on them using food coloring, add a string, and hang them on the tree. To this day, the scent of marshmallows makes me think of Christmas.

We salvaged scraps of colored construction paper from school projects to make balls and stars and candy canes to add to the tree. Red, green, and white paper strips made colorful chains. The star at the top was yellow construction paper.

When we were done, we had a tree that brought promises of Christmas treasure and joy to our hearts. We were completely satisfied with it, sitting there on the table in the dining room/parlor.

Even though money was tight for my parents, they always found a way to give us Christmas gifts. But we didn't find them wrapped and waiting under the tree. For one thing, there wouldn't have been room. For another, I can't see my parents wasting money on wrapping paper just to have it thrown away.

Usually on Christmas morning, Dad would come in from his shop carrying a big cardboard box he'd kept hidden ever since it arrived in the mail. Inside would be our gifts. We were just as thrilled with them as we would have been if they had been waiting for us under our tree.

When our own children were little, we had a ritual we followed strictly after we'd finished decorating our fresh and fragrant tree each year. We'd clean up the mess we'd made, and then I'd step back and say, "This is the most beautiful tree we've ever had!" If I forgot to say it, my son would prompt me.

I hope my children will remember those trees with as much nostalgia and love as I do the little bottlebrush tree of my own childhood.

Irises struggle to bloom in Neuberg Cemetery
near author's childhood home.

A Beloved Sacred Place

The small rural church building where I attended services as a child was moved years ago to a nearby farm and converted into a hen house. But the churchyard, a few acres along a graveled road in southeastern South Dakota, is still maintained because of the cemetery that fills half the space.

Tombstones—some ornate marble, some simple cement markers—are surrounded by weedy grass, kept mowed by a descendant of a family buried there. Along a barbed wire fence which separates the graveyard from a cornfield, irises struggle to survive, too stunted from regular mowing to bloom. Cedar trees grow protectively over a cluster of graves in one corner. Peony bushes planted decades ago on two or three graves bloom each spring.

Driving by, a person might think no one, except the diligent mower, ever visits this old cemetery. But one hot, windy day a few summers ago, I returned to stand in the shade of the cedars and reflect on what this location had meant to me and the families who built the little wooden church over a hundred years before.

That church, visited one Sunday in four by a circuit pastor, brought the surrounding neighborhood together each week. One of the older men read a sermon in German on Sundays when the pastor wasn't there.

At nine o'clock every Sunday morning, the women hustled their children inside for Sunday School. We children sat in the front rows of hard wooden chairs while our moms, some carrying infants, settled into chairs behind us, all on the left side of the center aisle. The men stayed outside—in cars during the winter, in the shade on the west side of the building in the summer—and visited.

After Sunday School, the men trooped in and sat on the right side of the aisle. I remember the stir caused by one young woman who, after being away at college several years, returned and sat on the men's side with her fiancé. But separate sides for separate genders continued in spite of her brave rejection of tradition.

In some ways, that church was like a local newspaper. You learned neighborhood news each Sunday as people lingered after the service to visit. If someone was missing, you found out why. Women shared news of their gardens and families; men discussed crops and hog or cattle prices.

Almost everyone in church was related to everyone else. We were a big, loving family that cared what was happening in each life—and made it our business to know just what that might be. Each

Sunday, we felt a warmth that can come only from knowing we were an important part of a community.

Standing beneath the gnarled cedars in that little old churchyard that summer day, I once again felt part of something special. Memories of family love, strong traditions, and unquestioning faith came whispering back to me on gusty prairie breezes. The church building is gone; the graves are mostly forgotten. But that little rural church lives on in the hearts of people for whom it was once a beloved sacred place.

BACHELOR BUTTON

ORDER FORM

ONLINE:

- Prairie Hearth Publishing, LLC:
  www.prairiehearthpublishingllc.com

- Amazon.com

ORDERS:

- Marilyn Kratz, 2007 Ross Street, Yankton, SD 57078
  605-664-5864
  mkratz@iw.net

Please send *Feed Sack Dresses and Wild Plum Jam* **to:**

Name _____

Address _____

City _____State_____

Zip _____ Telephone: (   ) _____

Book Price: $12.72 in U.S. dollars (includes tax)
Shipping: $3.00 for first book; $1.00 for each additional book
to cover shipping and handling to the U.S., Canada, and
Mexico. International orders: $4.00 for the first book and $1.50
for each additional book
Kindle version available at Amazon.com

*Quantity discounts available for orders
of 3 or more books. Please call* **605-664-5864.**

4548557R00072

Made in the USA
San Bernardino, CA
24 September 2013